FANTASTICALLY GREAT WOMEN WHO SAVED the PLANET

Kate Pankhurst

BLOOMSBURY
CHILDREN'S BOOKS
LONDON   OXFORD   NEW YORK   NEW DELHI   SYDNEY

Save our **fantastically** great planet with ...

Eugenic Clark

Wangari Maathai

INGEBORG BELING

ANITA RODDICK

EDITH FARKAS

Jane Goodall

ISATOU CEESAY

FLORENCE AUGUSTA MERRIAM BAILEY

MÁRÍÁ TELKES

Daphne Sheldrick

EILEEN KAMPAKUTA BROWN AND EILEEN WANI WINGFIELD

URSULA MARVIN

THE CHIPKO MOVEMENT

SAY NO to the DUMP

How did
they use their skills
and voices to look after our
marvellously beautiful world?

The women in this book knew that all life
on Earth deserves our respect and protection.
They dived deep into dangerous waters to study
man-eating sharks and cared for wild elephants orphaned
by poaching. When the world around them was threatened
by pollution or deforestation, they stood tall and spoke
up for what is right. They made scientific breakthroughs
that are helping to protect our planet's future and showed
that even small changes can make a BIG difference.

And VERY importantly, they sowed seeds of
change in others and inspired them to see
they had the power to save the planet too ...
just like YOU do!

Dive into ocean discovery with ...

Eugenie Clark

I travelled to TROPICAL oceans to study fish. I had to ignore lots of people who told me this was too DANGEROUS for a girl.

Eugenie became well known for the **INCREDIBLE SCIENTIFIC DISCOVERIES** she made, and the **ADVENTURES** she had making them!

Eugenie Clark's **FASCINATION** with sea creatures began in the early **1930s**, when she was just nine years old. Eugenie's mother needed something for her daughter to do while she went to work on Saturday mornings. One day, she dropped Eugenie off at the nearby **New York City Aquarium**. Eugenie was **HOOKED!**

She returned every Saturday, exploring **DEEPER** and **DEEPER** into underwater worlds.

"I brought my face as close as possible to the glass and pretended I was walking on the bottom of the sea."

Eugenie went on to become a **MARINE BIOLOGIST** and learned to **SCUBA DIVE**. This was a very unusual career for a woman at the time.

Never out of her depth, Eugenie studied creatures considered so **DEADLY** they should be avoided at all costs ...

SHARKS!

"people generally thought sharks were DUMB eating machines. I began to realise that these GANGSTERS OF THE DEEP had gotten a bad rep."

In the **1950s**, Eugenie successfully trained a nurse shark to hit a target. This showed that sharks are intelligent creatures.

In **1973**, Eugenie observed sharks that appeared to 'sleep' in an underwater cave in Mexico. Previously people thought that all species of shark had to swim at all times to breathe.

"The sea should be ENJOYED and the animals in it. When you see a SHARK you should say, 'How LUCKY I am'."

In 1981, a brave Eugenie hitched a ride on a passing 50-foot-long whale shark!

Eugenie made her last dive in **2014** – she was **92** years old!

Eugenie became known as the 'SHARK LADY'. She inspired people around the world to learn about our oceans and to respect ALL underwater creatures EQUALLY.

Wangari Maathai

Wangari Maathai grew up in the 1940s in the BEAUTIFUL landscape of Kenya. It was a place rich in natural wonders but it was not a wealthy country. Many people struggled to make enough money to feed their families. The government did little to help.

Wangari loved learning, it allowed her to grow. But at that time it was quite unusual for girls to go to school. So, in 1960, she left her home and took up an opportunity to study in the USA. But Wangari always felt rooted to Kenya's ...

I was the first woman from East Africa to get a PhD.

lush forests ... rustling leaves ... and streams that bubbled through the trees ...

When Wangari moved back to Kenya the landscape had changed ...

Trees were DISAPPEARING!

The government was cutting down forests to make room for crops worth lots of money, like coffee. This is called **DEFORESTATION**. Without trees, things started to go very wrong ...

With no trees to trap water, streams have trickled away.

The soil is like DUST!

We can't grow crops!

Something must be done! The cost to the environment is too high.

The government didn't like Wangari helping women to feel **powerful**. It wasn't used to anybody questioning what it did. Wangari faced threats and barriers to her work but she **REFUSED** to be **CUT DOWN**.

Things are GROWING well!

In **1977**, Wangari started the **Green Belt Movement**. She taught people about how their actions can hurt the environment. Communities were encouraged to work together to plant new trees. **Wangari put women in charge!** With each new seed that was planted, **IDEAS** grew too ...

Wangari's movement has helped over 900,000 women sow seeds of change. Over 51 million trees have been planted.

We won't let any more TREES be chopped down!

I don't like the way the country is run!

We DO have the POWER to change our lives.

In 2002, Kenya's government finally changed and Wangari joined the new team so she could help them to protect the environment. In 2004, Wangari was awarded the Nobel Peace Prize for her incredible work.

The Green Belt Movement continues to plant trees in Kenya and think of ideas and ways to tackle the threat of deforestation around the world.

INGEBORG

In Germany in the late 1920s, Ingeborg Beling helped to reveal the secret of what keeps all life on Earth ticking.

Ingeborg joined a team of scientists who noticed that bees did some **extraordinary things**. At the time some people mistakenly assumed bees were just chaotic insects, whose main ability was to make honey from nectar. However, Ingeborg proved that these **hard-working** little insects had another **astonishing** ability ...

We Can TELL the TIME!

INGEBORG'S EXPERIMENT:

Ingeborg wanted to see if she could train a hive of bees to expect food. She left food out for the bees between 4 p.m. and 6 p.m. Then she watched and waited ...

BEES!

4:00 p.m.
Tick, tock.

TUM TE TUM...

1:00 p.m.
Tick, tock.

Tick, tock.
6:30 a.m.

NO BEES.

I painted the BEES with different coloured SPOTS so they could be easily tracked and RECOGNISED!

Ingeborg gave us sugared water that smelt like lavender.

This just tasted just like the NECTAR we collect from FLOWERS.

BELING

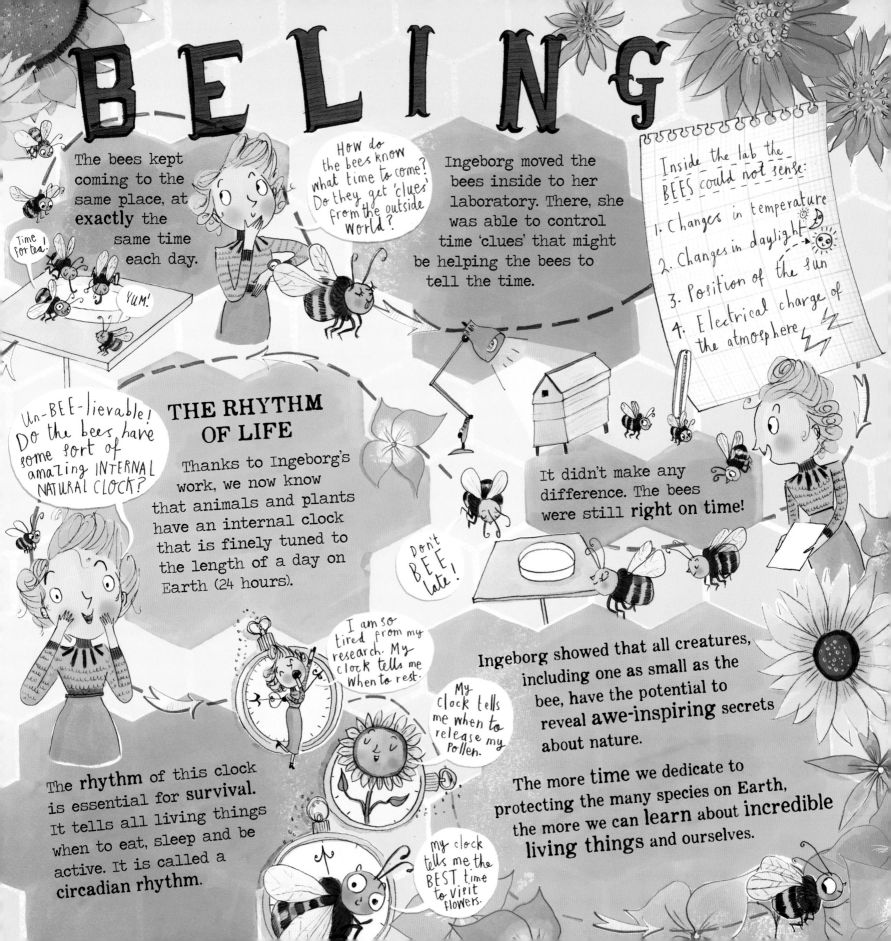

The bees kept coming to the same place, at **exactly** the same time each day.

Time for tea!

YUM!

How do the bees know what time to come? Do they get 'clues' from the outside world?

Ingeborg moved the bees inside to her laboratory. There, she was able to control time 'clues' that might be helping the bees to tell the time.

Inside the lab the BEES could not sense:
1. Changes in temperature
2. Changes in daylight
3. Position of the sun
4. Electrical charge of the atmosphere

Un-BEE-lievable! Do the bees have some sort of amazing INTERNAL NATURAL CLOCK?

THE RHYTHM OF LIFE

Thanks to Ingeborg's work, we now know that animals and plants have an internal clock that is finely tuned to the length of a day on Earth (24 hours).

Don't BEE late!

It didn't make any difference. The bees were still **right on time!**

I am so tired from my research. My clock tells me when to rest.

My clock tells me when to release my pollen.

The **rhythm** of this clock is essential for **survival**. It tells all living things when to eat, sleep and be active. It is called a **circadian rhythm**.

my clock tells me the BEST time to visit flowers.

Ingeborg showed that all creatures, including one as small as the bee, have the potential to reveal **awe-inspiring** secrets about nature.

The more time we dedicate to protecting the many species on Earth, the more we can **learn** about **incredible living things** and ourselves.

ANITA RODDICK

"If you do things well, do them BETTER. Be DARING, be FIRST, be DIFFERENT, be JUST."

Anita Roddick believed the best way to do business was to put kindness, people and the planet above simply making money. In 1976, in Brighton, UK, she opened The Body Shop. Anita made her own beauty products using natural, nurturing ingredients.

At the time, most companies tested things like shampoo, bubble bath and make-up on animals before they sold them. These animals suffered horrible injuries.

This is a NEW way to shop.

STOP ANIMAL TESTING!

Testing beauty products on animals was banned in the UK in 1998, and across the European Union in 2013. Anita campaigned for this cruel practice to end.

Body Shop products have NEVER and will NEVER be tested on animals!

The Body Shop was also one of the first companies to ...

BUY FAIR TRADE!

Anita used ingredients from around the world, including shea butter and Brazil nut oil. She ensured that farmers in poor communities could earn a decent living by paying them a **fair price**.

This means women like me can feed our families.

HELP SAVE THE ENVIRONMENT!

Anita raised awareness of serious environmental issues. She encouraged customers to think differently. Posters and packaging around the shop displayed strong messages about things like ...

extinct is forever

DEFORESTATION and ...

ENDANGERED ANIMALS.

animals in danger.

SAVE THE RAINFOREST

BAN AGAINST ANIMAL TESTING

I want to change things for the BETTER!

What I buy really can make a HUGE difference.

RECYCLE!

REFILL HERE

At the time, few people knew how important it is to reduce waste by recycling plastics. Anita gave customers the choice to refill their containers, rather than buying a new one each time. Now, The Body Shop recycle customers' empty pots and bottles instead.

Sadly, Anita died in 2007, but the way she did business has continued to inspire many other companies to work in ways that protect people and the planet.

THE SKY-GAZING SCIENTIST EDITH FARKAS

Edith Farkas was a meteorologist – a scientist who studies the weather. She looked up, up, up all the way through the sky to the ozone layer, which is the part of the atmosphere that protects life on Earth from the Sun's harmful rays. Edith's work was very important because it helped scientists to see that Earth could be facing an environmental disaster.

Start here.

I used a special instrument called a DOBSON SPECTROPHOTOMETER to get PRECISE measurements.

ANTARCTICA

NEW HORIZONS

Edith was born in Hungary in 1921, but came to New Zealand as a refugee during World War II. Although she'd already trained to be a scientist before she moved, her qualifications weren't recognised in New Zealand and she had to go back to university! But she didn't give up …

WEATHER WATCH

In 1953, Edith was one of the only female meteorologists working in New Zealand. Her job was to track changes to the thickness of the ozone layer. At the time, this was used to predict patterns and changes in the Earth's weather and temperature.

UP through the ATMOSPHERE

Sun

SPACE

ozone

STORM CLOUDS GATHER ...

In the 1980s the observations Edith had made for almost 30 years helped other scientists to see how much the ozone layer had changed over time. Due to pollution from man-made *CFC gases it was dramatically t-h-i-n-n-i-n-g over Antarctica. (This thinning was often referred to as the 'hole' in the ozone layer.)

Where the ozone layer is thinner, living things on Earth are more likely to be be exposed to the Sun's damaging UV rays and develop illness.

*CFC GASES were found in aerosol sprays and refrigerators.

A FROZEN FIELD TRIP

In 1975, Edith travelled to Antarctica to get a different look at the ozone layer. She was the first Hungarian woman and the first female meterologist from New Zealand to step foot on the continent.

Closely observing our planet over time can reveal unexpected and important things...

THE ANTARCTIC

A BRIGHTER OUTLOOK

To stop the ozone layer from becoming more damaged, countries all came together and took **drastic action.** The use of CFCs was **banned.** It showed that when countries work together to reduce pollution **incredible** things **can** happen ...

Today the OZONE over ANTARCTICA is in much better shape.

Small changes can threaten wildlife.

The environment is DELICATE.

Edith's ozone research showed that watching changes to our planet over time is essential to protecting it for future generations.

SHE CHANGED THE WAY WE THINK ABOUT CHIMPANZEES, AND OURSELVES ...

Jane Goodall

Jane was born in the UK in **1934**. As a child she was fascinated by animals and her favourite childhood toy was a chimpanzee called Jubilee. In **1960**, aged 26, Jane travelled to **Gombe Stream Chimpanzee Reserve** in Tanzania, to research **real-life wild chimpanzees**.

Chimps are known to be humans' closest relative but are often not seen as important enough to be protected from threats like **hunting** and **deforestation**. Unlike other scientists, who were mostly men, Jane had not been to university to learn the 'proper' way to study chimpanzees. This meant that she studied them using her own methods, which led to her making **extraordinary discoveries** ...

JANE'S FIELD NOTES:
Scientists usually number each animal they study but the chimps are **UNIQUE INDIVIDUALS** and they deserve names, not numbers! It is clear that they do many things that, up until now, scientists thought only humans were capable of.

DAVID GREYBEARD:
The first chimp to trust me enough to get close and to be seen using **TOOLS**.

I can use grass as a tool to catch **TERMITES!**

FLO:
She and her children taught me how **SIMILAR** chimp and human families are.

I CLEVERLY tricked other chimps by leading them away from food so I could eat it all.

We have close family bonds and look after each other.

FIGAN (Flo's son):
He showed me how chimps use their **INTELLIGENCE** in some very surprising ways!

At first, many scientists refused to take me seriously. They weren't used to the idea that any animal other than a human could have a personality, feelings or do complicated tasks.

Everything changed in **1965**, when a film about my work, called *Miss Goodall and the Wild Chimpanzees*, was shown on TV. My research was accepted and I became a **LEADING CHIMPANZEE EXPERT.**

They are just like humans – happy, joyful, angry.

Jane revealed how strikingly **similar** humans and chimps are. This helped people to understand that chimpanzees are our equals and deserve our respect and protection.

The Jane Goodall Trust, founded in 1977, carries out vital research and protects chimpanzees and their habitats. Now in her eighties, Jane still travels the world speaking out for the rights of our closest relatives on planet Earth.

"The least I can do is SPEAK out for those who cannot speak for themselves."

ISATOU CEESAY

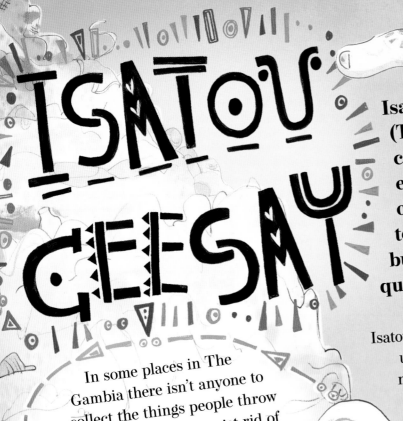

Isatou Ceesay grew up in The Gambia. (The Gambia is a poor, *developing country where very few children, especially girls, have the chance of a good education.) Isatou had to leave school at a young age but this did not stop her asking questions or solving BIG problems.

Look at this MESS!

In some places in The Gambia there isn't anyone to collect the things people throw away. With no way to get rid of them, the piles of plastic bags grew **bigger** and **bigger**.

Isatou noticed that people had stopped using woven baskets made from natural materials and were using plastic bags for their shopping. She also noticed that this was creating a very messy problem ...

In *developing countries lots of changes need to happen to give people the chance of a good job and a better quality of life.

Isatou discovered that waste plastic bags were causing lots of problems ...

Mosquitoes gather in water on bags and spread disease.

Animals eat the bags and get ill.

PLASTIC BAGS TAKE AROUND 1,000 YEARS TO DECOMPOSE.

In 1997, with help from an American organisation called the Peace Corps, Isatou came up with a clever plan ...

WOMEN! Your skills should not go to WASTE!

Isatou showed women how to **recycle** waste plastic bags into **beautiful** objects they could sell, like handbags and purses.

Over almost **20** years, more and more women from other villages got involved. Today over **2,000** women in **40** different communities are involved in what is now called the **Women's Initiative in The Gambia.**

In **2015**, The Gambia's government banned plastic bags. People are now encouraged to take their own re-usable bag to the shops and markets.

"In order to LOVE the environment you must first LOVE yourself."

making something valuable from rubbish is called UPCYCLING.

What we throw away can be BEAUTIFUL.

I am making a difference.

I want to look after the place I live.

Now I can afford to send my children to school.

For the first time I have my own money and a bank account.

We can help our country to DEVELOP!

Isatou's plan didn't just help **reduce the damage** rubbish causes to the environment – it also taught women **skills** that helped them become more **independent.**

The plastic problem is a lot better!

Isatou showed that by working and learning together, small groups can make **BIG** changes to their **lives** and the **environment.**

WATCHER, LOVER AND PROTECTOR OF BIRDS
FLORENCE AUGUSTA MERRIAM BAILEY

Florence Augusta Merriam Bailey was one of the first people to encourage others to learn about the wonders of WILD birds. This was a very new way of thinking in the late 1800s in the USA. At the time scientists didn't really observe birds in the wild.

Florence's new way of thinking came at a time when birds faced a huge threat from ... LADIES' FASHION! Shockingly, an estimated FIVE MILLION wild birds were killed each year – all so women could wear elaborate feathered decorations, and even whole stuffed birds, on their HATS.

In 1885, aged 19, Florence went to study at a ladies' college. She was HORRIFIED by the fashion choices of her fellow students ...

Eeep!

Women wore our Plumes!

SQUAWK!

stuffed humming birds were used on jewellery.

BEAUTIFULLY FEATHERED FANCY HATS!

so chic!

I love my hat.

They don't understand the DEVASTATION their hats are causing. I must show them.

Florence firmly believed that if more people knew how INTERESTING LIVING BIRDS were, far fewer would be needlessly killed.

STEPS TO CHANGE THE BEHAVIOUR OF THE COMMON FEATHERED-HAT-WEARING LADY

1. Ruffle feathers.

WEARING FEATHERS IS CRUEL TO BIRDS

GASP!

I didn't realise.

2. Start a new flock.

One third of students joined the society.

JOIN the AUDUBON SOCIETY Learn to love WILD BIRDS

3. Observe the ladies in their new habitat.

I organised nature walks with members to see wild birds.

WOW! WOW! LOOK!

BIRDS THROUGH AN OPERA GLASS

TWEET.

1889

A-BIRDING ON A BRONCO

I bird-watched on my horse Billy in California USA.

1896

Florence spent the rest of her life hiking and camping across the USA RESEARCHING BIRDS. She published some of the first ever GUIDES TO BIRD-WATCHING and APPRECIATING NATURE that were aimed at ordinary people.

FLORENCE'S BIRDWATCHING TIPS

1. Avoid light or bright-coloured clothing.

2. Walk slowly and noiselessly.

3. Stop often, listen for bird song.

BIRDS I HAVE SEEN:

Florence's books and campaigning played a huge role in changing people's attitudes towards birds. By 1900, laws had been passed to stop the trade in bird feathers. Eventually the fashion for feathered hats was no longer considered acceptable.

MÁRIA TELKES

She became known as **'the Sun Queen'** for her solar-powered ideas!

WOW!

It looks so warm!

In the 1940s in the USA, Hungarian **INVENTOR** and scientist Mária Telkes developed technology using one of the world's **BRIGHTEST** planet-saving ideas – solar energy!

This had been Mária's **DREAM** since her teenage years when she read a book about the **FUTURE OF POWER**. She was intrigued by a new scientific idea – could technology be invented to turn the sun's energy into power for our homes, travel and everyday lives? Scientists were interested in this idea because solar energy is free and *RENEWABLE.

At the time, there had been a few experiments into **SOLAR ENERGY**. Nobody had managed to invent a system that could transform our everyday lives. Mária changed all that ...

Renewable energy comes from sources that won't run out like the SUN, WAVES AND WIND. Using renewables means we can use fewer polluting FOSSIL FUELS to make energy.

*Fossil Fuels like COAL, OIL AND GAS are burned to make energy. The POLLUTION this releases is causing the planet to heat up – this is known as GLOBAL WARMING. Today we know this is changing our weather and affecting wildlife. Countries are now urgently working towards a FUTURE OF RENEWABLE ENERGY.

My INVENTION was a solar-heated house. I worked with some other AMAZING women to build it ...

MÁRIA'S TEAM

I was from a RICH family and DONATED money to SCIENTIFIC WONDERS.

Toasty warm.

ELEANOR RAYMOND: ARCHITECT

I wanted to build homes for the FUTURE.

AMELIA PEABODY: FUNDER

THE DOVER SUNHOUSE

The first of its kind, built in **1948**, the Dover Sunhouse was heated entirely using solar technology! At the time scientists knew that fossil fuels would run out one day and were concerned about how soon that would happen. It was also a period when many ordinary people struggled to afford to heat their homes. All this led to Mária's pioneering vision for a **home of the future** ...

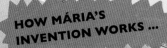

HOW MÁRIA'S INVENTION WORKS ...

Specially-designed **HUGE** windows **absorb warmth** from the sun ...

Warm air is blown by fans into metal drums filled with a **special type of salt** ...

When warmed, **the salt melted which meant it stored heat** ...

In **cooler** weather, the salt **hardened** and released its stored heat into the house.

Have you ever seen anything like it?

In all my years NEVER!

"Each new house is a stepping stone towards the use of the sun as a fuel resource"

Mária's experiment showed that solar technology had **HUGE** potential. This was an important step towards **USING** environmentally-friendly sources of energy.

Scientists have developed Mária's ideas over the years and today **SOLAR ENERGY** is the fastest-growing renewable clean energy source around the globe. But the search for ways to make solar technology **AFFORDABLE** for as many homes as possible continues ...

It's like living in the FUTURE!

PURRRR

AMAZING SCIENCE!

We can INVENT more solar technology!

Standing with nature ... THE CHIPKO MOVEMENT

In the **1960s**, the Indian government began allowing logging companies to chop down countless trees in the forests of the Indian Himalayas. Without the trees to protect the soil there were **disastrous** floods and landslides.

Women in the area were traditionally in charge of looking after children and providing food. When crops and houses were **swept away**, women's lives were very badly affected.

In **1973**, women of **Lata Village** heard about a local campaigner called Chandi Prasad Bhatt. He wanted villagers to protest by standing in the way of loggers and **hugging the trees**. (The Indian word meaning 'to hug' or 'to cling to' is **chipko**.)

At that time in India, men took care of problems affecting village life. To some people the idea of a group of women making such a stand was considered **outrageous**.

This did not stop the women, who knew their survival depended on the trees. They **embraced** the idea of **peaceful protest** ...

The loggers carry guns.

Don't be afraid.

I will give my life before these trees are cut down! They are as important as my mother's home or 'maika'. (A place precious in Indian culture.)

Out of our way!

The loggers could not chop down any trees and had no choice but to **leave**. The unusual news of very poor women making such a **powerful protest** rustled through the leaves ...

SAVE the TREES!

... to the **government**. They investigated and listened to local people. A ban was placed on logging in the area for the next **TEN YEARS**.

The news also reached other women affected by **deforestation**. More and more women in the region took part in Chipko protests. Many more trees were saved by temporary bans on logging. The **CHIPKO MOVEMENT** had **taken hold!**

Calmness speaks LOUDER than shouting.

They are SO BRAVE!

Women from nearby villages supported us.

We did not move for FOUR days.

Our protests were called a MOVEMENT because they spread from village to village.

HUMPH!

By **standing strong** with the ancient trees that kept their way of life safe, women were able to reduce deforestation and protect their lands from floods. For the first time, women could have their say about looking after the environment they lived in.

The **natural resources** of the Indian Himalayan forests continue to face threats from logging. Protests **inspired** by the **brave actions** of the original Chipko women are still happening today.

Dreaming of a better future ...

EILEEN KAMPAKUTA BROWN AND EILEEN WANI WINGFIELD

In the 1990s, *Aboriginal elders, Eileen Kampakuta Brown and Eileen Wani Wingfield led a brave campaign to stop the government building a *nuclear waste dump close to their desert home in Woomera, South Australia.

Eileen and Eileen had seen their land poisoned once before. In the 1950s, it was used as a test site for nuclear weapons. Aboriginal people weren't told that the testing was unsafe, and many of them became very ill.

This time Eileen and Eileen had something to say ...

Although *Nuclear power stations produce far less air pollution than other types of power station, and don't burn natural resources, the nuclear waste they produce can remain dangerous to humans and wildlife for 10,000 years.

*Aboriginal people lived in Australia for thousands of years before anyone else settled there. Their culture is one of the oldest in the world.

Our home is HOT and DRY but it is ALIVE with nature, songs and the ANCIENT stories of our ancestors.

These stories are called the DREAMING.

"IRATI WANTI!"
(This means—THE POISON! LEAVE IT!)

What if something goes wrong? We don't want our land POISONED!

WOOMERA

Eileen and Eileen helped to form the **Kupa Piti Kungka Tjuta**, a group of Aboriginal elder women determined to protect their home ...

They travelled by bus for **days at a time** to protest, camping out in the cold.

They went to the **2000 Olympic Games** in Sydney and all the way to Parliament House in Canberra.

In 2003, Eileen and Eileen received the **Goldman Environmental Prize** for their incredible work.

In 2004, the Australian government was forced to abandon its plan for the dump. Eileen and Eileen's campaign played a huge part in making this happen. Sadly, **Aboriginal land** is still under threat as the search continues to find a place to put the dump.

Eileen Kampakuta Brown died in 2012, and Eileen Wani Wingfield in 2014. The conversations they started about preserving the environment for future generations, whatever their way of life, are still going on today.

DISCOVER THE SECRETS OF THIS WORLD AND OTHERS WITH ...

URSULA MARVIN

In the USA during the **1940s**, Ursula Marvin learned that rocks hold clues to the **DRAMATIC FORCES** that made the Earth **BILLIONS** of years ago. From that moment, Ursula knew she wanted to become a **GEOLOGIST**. (Geologists study the materials our planet is made from.)

LOOKING at the structure of rocks can help us to understand the forces that shape Earth today— like earthquakes and volcanoes.

Few women worked as geologists but Ursula didn't let this hold her back. She became an expert in ... **OUTER SPACE!**

I ♥ ROCKS

At university my professor told me I should learn to cook instead!

I started to study space rocks in the 1950s during the SPACE RACE— a time when the USA wanted to be the first to uncover the secrets of space.

A space rock that lands on Earth is called a ...

METEORITE
(Large rocks that are still in space are called **ASTEROIDS**.)

In **1969**, Ursula helped to make important discoveries about samples of rock from **NASA's** Apollo missions to the **MOON**.

In the **1970s**, Ursula became the first ever woman to go **meteorite hunting** in Antarctica! Meteorites that fell from space millions of years ago have sunk below the surface of the ice. They are carried along, trapped in the slow-moving ice, until clusters of them reappear on the surface.

METEORITE STRIKES are very rare. In **1982**, Ursula went to investigate a **STRANGE** incident involving a meteorite that may have come from **space**.

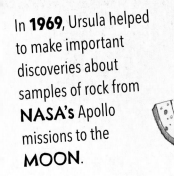

TWO METEORITES HIT SAME TOWN!

Scientists today are continuing Ursula's work to protect our planet from **IMPENDING DOOM!** They want to learn more about **ASTEROIDS** in space and think this could help them to divert any large **METEORITES** from hitting Earth in the future.

Ursula died in **2018**. To remember the **DISCOVERIES** she made about our world and others, a **MOUNTAIN PEAK** in the Arctic and an **ASTEROID** have been named after her.

Whoosh!

Daphne Sheldrick

Born to British parents in 1934, Daphne Sheldrick grew up in Kenya. Daphne loved Africa's amazing wildlife and knew how important it was to preserve it. So, in the 1960s, Daphne and her husband David helped set up Tsavo National Park (a large area of land that is specially protected). The Sheldricks were a very unique sort of family – they shared their home with countless wild animals!

Daphne loved all the animals, but it was the young elephants that made the **BIGGEST** footprint on her heart. Tragically, poachers had hunted their parents for their ivory tusks. (Some people see ivory as a valuable material and use it to make trinkets and, at one time, piano keys.) Daphne spent the next 60 years doing all she could to help orphaned elephants.

She discovered that elephants experience **POWERFUL EMOTIONS**, just as humans do.

They feel ... **SADNESS** ...

Rhinos also lost their parents to poachers who wanted their horn.

I love my life in the garden.

JOY ...

It took young orphans a long time to recover from the HORRIBLE shock of losing their parents.

We live in Daphne's garden.

My BELOVED Eleanor left to join a WILD herd, but she always recognised me afterwards.

An elephant never forgets those who helped them.

Daphne was the first person to discover a MILK recipe suitable for NEWBORN elephants – a mix of cow's milk and coconut milk. Before this, it was hard for them to survive without their mum.

Around 200 young elephants were saved by Daphne. She was always sad to see her elephants leave, but she knew the WILD was where their true home was.

LOVE!
One elephant developed a really special bond with Daphne.

My name is ELEANOR.

Eleanor is EXTRAORDINARY. She knew I was trying to save orphans and helped me to look after them.

Daphne took action against the danger elephants faced from poachers and farming, which destroys their habitat. Her brilliant work was given special recognition. This included being made a dame by the Queen of England and receiving Kenya's highest honour, Moran of the Burning Spear.

Daphne died in 2018, aged 83. Her amazing work in Kenya carries on through the charity she founded, THE SHELDRICK WILDLIFE TRUST.

Elephants have suffered at the hands of humans but can still FORGIVE even though they can't FORGET.

STUPENDOUS SAV
There is so much to DISCOVER about ocean life.
Turn TRASH into TREASURE!
PROTECT THE PLANET FOR FUTURE GENERATIONS!
Give our planet a BRIGHTER OUTLOOK.
STAND TALL, stand together.
How will you SPEAK UP
You can help people to understand and LOVE nature.

FANTASTICALLY GREAT WORDS

Aboriginal people who lived in Australia before others settled there. Their culture is one of the oldest in the world

Asteroid a large chunk of rock and metal in space that orbits the Sun

Atmosphere a layer of gases that surrounds and protects the Earth

CFC gases used to be found in solvents, refrigerants and aerosol sprays

Chipko a Hindi word meaning 'to hug' or 'to cling to'

Circadian rhythm the name given to the 'internal body clock' of animals and plants

Cruelty-free products that are not tested on or do not cause harm to animals

Deforestation the action of clearing a wide area of trees

Developing country a country where lots of changes need to happen to give people a better quality of life

Dreaming stories, art, songs and ceremonies that explain the workings of the universe, as well as the history and traditions of Aboriginal people

Endangered animals or plants at serious risk of extinction

Fair trade when farmers and workers are paid a fair price for the goods they produce

Fossil fuels are formed from the remains of ancient plants and animals buried deep in the earth, such as coal, oil and natural gas

Global warming describes how the Earth is heating up because of human activities

Ivory the material that elephant tusks are made from

Logging cutting down trees to sell

Meteorite a space rock that lands on Earth

NASA stands for National Aeronautics and Space Administration and the people who work there study outer space

National park a large area of land that is specially protected

Natural resources something that is found in nature and can be used by people

Nobel Prize a special award given every year to people who have done extraordinary things for the world

Nuclear power a powerful form of energy that can be dangerous if not used safely

Ozone layer the part of the atmosphere that protects us from the Sun's harmful rays

Poaching the illegal hunting, capturing or killing of animals

Pollution happens when the environment is damaged by waste, chemicals or other harmful things

Recycle taking old things and making them into something new

Refugee people who have had to leave their home because of war or a natural disaster and need a new, safe place to live

Renewable energy comes from sources that won't run out, like the Sun, waves and wind

Solar energy energy given off by the Sun, like light and heat

Space Race the competition between the USA and the Soviet Union (now Russia) to explore space in the 1950s/60s

UV rays waves of light from the Sun that can be harmful